Re-Defining

Manhood

Andreas Robert

<u>Book Tittle: Re Defining Manhood</u>

Cover Design by Valde Johannes

Layout by Avril Cordom

National Library, Namibia

Publisher: Self Publish

AUTHOR CONTACT DETAILS

Cellphone: +264 818361312

Email: chiefrobertofficial@gmail.com

Postal address: P O Box 24313, Windhoek, Namibia
Website: chiefrobertandreas.com

DEDICATION

This Book Is Entirely Dedicated To Every Boy Child and Father Figure Of Current and Future Generation (Unborn Generation).

ACKNOWLEDGMENT

First and foremost, I give all Glory and Honor to the Almighty God. As a vessel, I acknowledge the driving force of my life, which is Jesus Christ. Without Him, this book would not have been possible.

I extend my heartfelt gratitude to Ms. Liina Mutilifa for her invaluable technical support and contribution to this work. In loving memory of my Dad, Silvanus Andreas, whose presence in my life, along with my uncles, contributed to the foundation of this book.

I would also like to express my deep appreciation to Mrs. Cordom for aligning the book and providing technical assistance to get it published on Amazon. My sincere thanks to Mr. Valde Johannes for designing the cover.

I am profoundly honored to extend my deepest gratitude to two distinguished individuals who graciously contributed forewords to this book: Professor Peter Katjavivi whose unwavering dedication to empowering young men is a testament that permeates through these pages, and Prophet Philip Haindongo, whose spiritual guidance and steadfast support have greatly fortified my commitment to this mission.

I want to especially acknowledge the woman who carried me for nine months and still continues to carry me in her prayers Mrs Elizabeth Mweshipopya-Nehale. Thank you, Mom, for your unwavering love and support.

Finally, my last acknowledgment goes out to every boy child who will read this book and every parent who will use this book as guide to raise their child in a manner pleasing to God.

FORWARD

1. Professor Peter Katjavivi

Speaker of National Assembly (March 2015 –March 2025)

In a world that is rapidly changing, the essence of manhood seems to lately have become a contentious subject. The traditional values and roles that have defined manhood for generations are being challenged and redefined, leaving many to question what it truly means to be a man today. In "Re-Defining Manhood," Andreas Robert boldly tackles these pressing issues, providing a thoughtful exploration of the role of men in contemporary society.

As a politician and academic who has dedicated much of my life to public service and education, I recognize the profound impact that strong male leadership can have on families and communities. The importance of a father, a brother, a mentor, figures who embody integrity, responsibility, and humility-cannot be overstated. Yet, as Andreas highlights, we are witnessing a troubling trend: a decline in these essential qualities among men, often exacerbated by societal dynamics that have left many feeling adrift.

This book serves as a timely reminder that manhood is not merely a biological or social construct; it is a calling that requires to respect God's creation, a dedication to self-improvement, service to others, and a deep commitment to one's family and community. Andreas draws upon his own experiences, weaving in personal testimony and scriptural insights that resonate with both men and women alike. His reflections on biblical principles of manhood challenge us to embrace a more profound understanding of our roles as leaders, nurturers, and protectors.

Andreas's exploration is not only for those who seek to reassert their own identities but also serves as a guide for the younger generation, our boys, who must navigate the complexities of modern life. By presenting a clear vision of what it means to embody true manhood, he inspires hope for a future where men rise to fulfill their God-given potential, inherent of their creation as at birth.

In closing, I encourage you to engage with the ideas presented in this book with an open heart and mind. Let it be a catalyst for discussion, reflection, and action in your own life. Together, we can cultivate a generation of men who honor their responsibilities, nurture their families, and positively influence society.

Indeed, the idea of family values, parenthood and children's rights from abuse, exploitation and misuse. These are all values that are shared universally.

Prof. Peter Hitjitevi Katjavivi

Speaker of the National Assembly of Namibia

Chancellor, Namibian University of Science and Technology

March 2025

2. Prophet Phillip Haindongo

Founder and Overseer General Of EMC

It is with great reverence and a deep sense of responsibility that I present *Re Defining Manhood*, a prophetic work by Andreas Robert, which addresses the profound challenges faced by men in today's world. As the founder and overseer of Empowered Missionary of Christ Ministries, I have been privileged to witness the grace of God in guiding men back to His purpose. But in this age, where confusion often clouds the true essence of manhood, it is vital that we address this confusion from a biblical perspective, returning to the foundation that God established for men.

<u>Book Tittle: Re Defining Manhood</u>

In my years of ministry, I have encountered the silent pain of many men who, though walking among us, are burdened by deep spiritual and emotional struggles. It is heartbreaking to see so many of God's sons lost in despair, disconnected from their purpose and identity.

Re Defining Manhood is a prophetic call to all men to return to their rightful place in God's kingdom. We are called to be leaders, protectors, and providers, but above all, we are called to reflect God's glory in the earth. This book calls men to step into their true identity, to heal from past wounds, and to be restored to the fullness of the strength and dignity that God has ordained for them. Andreas Robert, drawing from personal experience and a profound understanding of biblical truth, speaks directly to the hearts of men, encouraging them to rise above societal pressures and embrace the divine purpose for which they were created.

<u>Book Tittle: Re Defining Manhood</u>

This book is not merely a guide for personal growth, but a message of divine empowerment. It is a prophetic tool, anointed to challenge the spirit of confusion and despair that has sought to strip men of their purpose. I urge every man, young and old, to take the time to engage with this work. Reflect on the qualities that define true manhood that are rooted in Christ: leadership, humility, responsibility, and service. We are living in a time when our nation, and indeed the world, desperately needs strong, righteous male role models.

This book is more than just words; it is a divine mandate for transformation. I pray that as you read, your heart will be stirred, your mind renewed, and your spirit restored. May *Re Defining Manhood* become a powerful tool in the hands of God's men, bringing healing, hope, and restoration to families, communities, and nations. Let us rise up and walk in the power, authority, and purpose that God has called us to.

May God bless you and empower you to fulfill His divine calling in your life.

In His service,

Prophet Philip Haindongo

Founder and Overseer General,

Empowered Missionary of Christ Ministries
March 2025

TABLE OF CONTENTS

Book Tittle: Re Defining Manhood

<u>Book Tittle: Re Defining Manhood</u>

INTRODUCTION

Re-Defining Manhood

This generation has lost the standards/dignity of manhood as laid by our ancestors. According to the bible: Biblical manhood is not just about strength or authority but it is about responsibility, integrity, and sacrificial love (1 Corinthians 16:13, Ephesians 5:25, Proverbs 20:7).

A true man leads with wisdom, protects with strength, and serves with humility. He is someone who builds, nurtures, and takes accountability for his actions. In today's world, manhood is often confused with dominance or success, but the Bible presents a deeper, more meaningful perspective.

The boy child or rather man, is supposed to be the head of the house. This has since been changed by the society we live in. Today women have taken the roles of being the head of the house and the man seat back and relax in their comfort. The boy child has lost the real definition and purpose of their existence.

In the present era, men have sold out their identities to women either knowingly or unknowingly. As such man have lost respect in their homes, marriages, workplaces, communities and the entire present generation. I refer to the present generation, because we have more women figures doing what man are supposed do especially in the leadership positions. Men have gone in hiding; though we have been appointed as natural leaders by God our stand in leadership positions are becoming extinct. The stereotype of man chase successful woman, can only further confirm that man have lost their dominion to the women. What is more pathetic is that, Man are comfortable with this stereotype, instead of taking up the challenge to better themselves, they have agreed with it. Women on the other hand have greatly accepted to go above the men. This was, however, not their wish, but it should be understood that a GAP, was left in society and should be filled. As such the Women took up the role to become leaders in society and their homes. Women filled the GAP, accepting what the universe have presented to them. Women occupied the space because the MAN is refusing to bring out their identity, leadership, authority and manhood in the society.

Presently, we do have a good number of male figures that have remained solid in society and have proven the role of a man, first at home, in the workplace and in the community. If you are the man that falls in the last category, I want you to continue doing what you are doing. The world need more of you.

The men of today have become criminals, thieves, women molester's, alcohol and drug abusers. What is even more unpleasant is man becoming women and they want to be accepted in the new absurd identity (LGBTQIA+ Community). Children are being raised in homes with absent fathers. As such society is being broken from the home level, because of poor family leadership demonstrated by man who is failing to be the head of the house.

This book will help you understand what Real Manhood is. This book will further guide you on how to restore and maintain your dignity as a man and head of the family as initially planned by God at the beginning of creation (Gensis 2:7). This book is also meant to usher and nurture the boy child into an ideal successful man with a character pleasing to God. The man was created first before a woman, giving him superiority.

The purpose of the man is provided to us in Gensis 2: 15-17.

The Lord God took the man and put him in the *Garden of Eden to work it and take care of it. 16 And the Lord God commanded the man, "You are free to eat from any tree in the garden; 17 but you must not eat from the tree of the knowledge of good and evil, for when you eat from it you will certainly die."*

The main purpose of the man is to work and take care of something. For example, in a marriage, a man must work and provide for his family. He is to take care of the family, to shield and protect the family, and to take care of his wife. All that was growing in the garden was blossoming because of Adams's hard work. He took care of all the plants; similarly, man should do the same. A man's garden is the family. Firstly, the man should water his flower which is the wife. The wife is the one who bears the fruits and remains the source of all the existing plants in the garden.

This book is an inspiration of the Holy Spirit as early as my Primary school years. As a child, I suffered emotional, mental, and physical trauma because of the condition I was brought up in. This almost made me lose my purpose in life if not for God's promises that are Yes and Amen 2nd Corinthians 1:20. I had to endure, so that I may be a living testimony today. To come and redefine manhood in a manner pleasing to God's purpose. This is My Purpose in Life. Since my Primary School years, the Lord has revealed to me things about how a man should be as opposed to my day-to-day experience. And it is exactly what this book is about. The God that revealed this to me, had the plan to Save an entire generation of Men in mind when he gave me the revelation. I kept on being reminded of this revelation until I took up the pen and paper and began the journey of writing this book.

The insights I received from God, combined with my life experiences, were reinforced by my undergraduate research for my first Bachelor of Education (B.Ed.) Honours qualification, as well as my theology degree from the Good News Theology School in the United States. These experiences have deepened my understanding of manhood from God's perspective.

This book is inspired by the Hope of Glory in Colossians 1:27, which is Jesus in me. The instructions in this book are not AGE-Bound. The powerful meditation in this book is not Time-Bound either. Are you the Joseph of your family? (Genesis 41:1-45) *"God favored Joseph and promoted him from a slave and prisoner to a*

Second Man-In-Command of Egypt". Be inspired by the spirit of God the Highest through the reading of this book and become the powerful and influential head of your family, the Chief Executive Officer (CEO), the Politician of your nation, and a Servant of God who not only shows the way but walks in the way pleasing to God.

If you've come this far, it's because the Spirit of the Lord has convicted you for a reason. Don't hesitate to read and finish this book, and your life will never be the same again.

Chapter meditation

1. Empty me of myself Lord Jesus and fill me with your spirit.

2. Cleanse me Lord that I may be pleased to enter your presence.

3. Fill me with wisdom that will allow me to make decisions with a positive impact on my family.
4. I am the Joseph of my family.
5. Help me Lord to be the man you created me to be.

CHAPTER 1

Understanding Manhood

"If boys don't learn, man will never know"

Manhood means servanthood. When you lose the selfish feeling of only thinking about yourself and you start to put those around you before yourself, then you have entered manhood. True manhood is about adding value to others' lives. Therefore, a man is first a servant. This is perfectly modeled in the life of Jesus Christ, who is a true reflection of what true manhood looks like. Jesus, though He was unlimited in power and incomprehensible in intellect, humbled Himself to become a man, until he suffered death on the cross for us. He endured not only physical pain but also spiritual anguish and the mockery of the world.

In the eyes of the world, Christ did not die an honorable or glorious death. He died in shame, in dishonor, and – though He claimed to be God and claimed to bring a new kingdom to the world – He was instead arrested, beaten, and killed. To all who watched the movie of the Passion of Christ and have read the scriptures. It appears that this man had a mission and has also failed in the most miserable and lowly ways possible. This of course is according to the wisdom of man.

But you and I know the truth. Did Jesus fail in His mission? Of course Not! His life was not marked by delusion, weakness, and failure, but rather by consistent humility, servanthood, and sacrifice brought him victory. This is our definition of manhood in this book (the characters of humility, servanthood, and sacrifice portrayed by a Man).

Christ exemplified Biblical Manhood. As a man of God, a head of your household, a big brother, and a male figure in your school or community, your call is to die to yourself and use your strength to stand up for your subordinates (the weak members of society). It's a call to seek the welfare of your family, your friends, and your neighbors before yourself.

Manhood is a call to imitate Jesus, even though we will never perfectly do this, we need to submit to Him as best as we can, trusting Him to empower us to live a life of service and worship.

Biblical manhood which is the ability to pursue godliness while retaining your masculinity is missing in the church, and the need for more godly men is necessary for the transformation of our governments, organizations, churches, and families. We need men to lead, protect, and provide both spiritually, physically, and financially (Merida, 2014).

Below Paul, an Apostle of Christ identifies Six Qualities of a Man of God. NB! As long as you are a Male figure, growing into becoming a man, you are a Man of God being referred to here by Apostle Paul.

Paul Six Virtues

1 Timothy 6: 11: But you, man of God,flee from all this, and pursue righteousness, godliness, faith, love, endurance and gentleness.

Paul gives six virtues that males should pursue to qualify to be categorized in the correct and biblical definition of manhood which are:

Righteousness, **Godliness**, **Faith**, **Love**, **Steadfastness**, and **Gentleness**. The imperative "pursue" is also a present-tense command. Every day we must follow after the above-mentioned virtues that flow from our union with Christ. Therefore, holiness is not just about abstaining from certain actions; it is about pursuing God, like a deer panting for water (Ps 42:1). ***Do not just say no to sin; say yes to God.***

Psalm 42: 1 As the deer pants for streams of water, so my soul pants for you, my God.

Follow after Righteousness

Righteousness means to possess a right relationship with God and people. Paul is not talking about self-imputed righteousness (the righteousness we receive at our justification). He is talking about practical righteousness. The man of God should hunger and thirst for righteousness (Matt 5:6). He will live with honesty before God and honesty before people. Be right with God, and be fair and just in your dealings with people.

Follow after Godliness

This virtue is closely related to righteousness. Godliness begins with a worshiping heart. Men of God love God and serve Him with a reverent fear (Heb 12:28). Consequently, men of God do not play around with sin; they kill sin. Again, the preacher must first pursue holiness before preaching it. John Flavel said, "Brethren, it is easier to declaim against a thousand sins of others than to mortify one sin in ourselves." Make sure you are a clean vessel.

Do not forget the culture of the inner man I mean of the heart. How diligently the cavalry officer keeps his saber clean and sharp; every stain he rubs off with the greatest care. Remember you are God's sword, His instrument a trusted chosen vessel unto Him to bear His name. In great measure, according to the purity and perfections of the instrument, will be the success. It is not great talents God blesses so much as great likeness to Jesus. A holy minister is a great weapon in the hands of God.

Follow after Faith

The man of God must trust God. We live by faith. MacArthur said, "To live a life of faith . . . is to live in a state of relaxed desperation. The man of God is desperate, because of the tremendous weight of responsibility his ministry entails, yet he is relaxed because of his confidence in the sovereignty of God." A high view of God is necessary for faithfulness and longevity in ministry.

Follow after Love

Instead of the youthful displays of bickering, impatience, and contentiousness, the man of God must love. You must care sincerely for the people of God if you are going to pastor them. Of course, there are times when you want to strike a blow, but you must refrain and remember the love that God had for you when you were unloved. Set to your people an example of genuine love for the body of Christ. Love them enough to wash their feet and love them enough to tell them the truth. Demonstrate a deep concern for the poor and the unreached peoples of the world, as well.

Follow after Steadfastness

The Man of God must endure to the end. The word endure means, "to bear up under, or remain under." The weight of ministry is demanding, but with the Spirit's help, we must persevere. Remember that the goal of our ministries is a lifetime of faithfulness, not sporadic faithfulness. There are times in which we fall, and by God's grace, get up again. This is further promised to us by the word of God.

Psalm 34: 19 Many are the afflictions of the righteous, But the Lord delivers him out of them all (NKJV)

Therefore, we should take the long view. Pursue longevity and endure all. Do not get carried away with big events invitation that last only but for a moment (weekend). Focus on the finishing line, like Jesus who endured until it was finished.

Follow after Gentleness

In Paul's requirements for the Pastor, he noted that the overseer should display gentleness, not violence (1 Tim 3:3). This concept carries the idea of strength under control. It does not mean "weakness." So, when the older woman comes up to you ten minutes before the sermon and asks, "Why is the homecoming not in the bulletin?" think before you respond. Let your word be FEW. Do not use the pulpit as a place for browbeating either. Remember Jesus was coupled in strength and authority with humility and meekness. He is the picture of Gentleness.

Chapter one prayer points and meditation

Prayer Points:

1. Lord, give me the heart of a servant. Teach me to lead by serving others, putting their needs before mine, and reflecting Your

humility in all that I do. In Jesus' name, Amen.

2. Father, help me to live a life that adds value to others. May I serve with integrity and love, just as Jesus served, and may my actions reflect His selflessness. In Jesus' name, Amen.

3. God, grant me the strength to serve others with humility and without seeking recognition. Let my life be a testimony of sacrificial love and service. In Jesus' name, Amen.

Declarations:

1. I declare that I am a servant of God, called to serve and uplift others. I choose to lead with humility and

sacrifice, following the example set by Christ.

2. I declare that my life will be a reflection of the selflessness and humility that Jesus demonstrated. I will seek to serve others and put their needs before my own.

3. I declare that I am a man of service. I will humble myself daily and embrace the role of servant-leader in every area of my life.

CHAPTER 2

Misconception of Manhood (manhood today)

"Men often overcompensate to prove and affirm their masculinity."

Growing up, I had been exposed to both negative and positive conceptions of manhood. But because God has chosen me for his purpose he kept me neutral and made sure that I don't fall but rather see both sides to come and redefine manhood and masculinity for his glory. Like most men who grew up without a father in the home, I was never taught by a man how to be a man; my manhood identity is inspired by the holy spirit for the sake of this message today. I learned to be a man the best way I could.

Men often overcompensate to prove and affirm their masculinity. Based on what I observed, I pretty much narrowed down manhood to the pursuit of five (5) things. I call these 5 things, "The 5 Misconceptions of Manhood. Allow me to quickly explain each:

1. Education

This is when we try to define our manhood by how smart we are; where we went to college/university; how many degrees we earn; and how much we know based on how much others don't know. In other words, if I'm smarter than you, then I must be a better man than you, right? This is Wrong! Overcompensation was me getting more degrees than a thermometer and earning a doctorate before I was 30 years old. **Manhood is not determined by how much a man "knows," but rather by how much he "grows" in wisdom as a man and how he uses his wisdom to impact the people around him.**

2. Occupation

This is defining manhood by what you do for a living; the title or position you hold or achieve (CEO, Doctor, President, Director, etc.). That's usually why the first thing a stranger usually asks you when you're on a plane is "What do you do?" Overcompensation for me in this area was becoming a business owner by age 22, a university graduate by age 25, and a published author by age 30. Are you starting to see a pattern here? Manhood is not determined by what man does, but rather by who a man is. We are human beings, not human "doings."

3. Compensation

This is when we define our manhood by how much money we make/earn; what we own; our net worth; and what and how much we can buy. More times than not, our level of education and our chosen occupation dictate this. At least for me, it did. Manhood is not determined by how much a man makes, but rather by how much of a difference a man makes in the lives of others. Income with no impact is wasteful.

4. Reputation

This is when we attempt to define manhood based on popularity, notoriety, and respect. How many people know us; follow us on Twitter, like us on Facebook; value what we have to say; desire to be us, be with us, or we can gain access to them? This speaks to our desire for "significance" – to be and feel important. For me, and a lot of men, I could attract, sleep with, and impress beautiful women. It was also me pursuing standing ovations and the praises from the people in my speaking audiences. Just think of awards, affirmation, and achievement. Authentic manhood is not defined by a man's reputation, but rather by his character. Reputation is who people think you are; character is who you are when nobody's looking.

5. Intimidation

This is when a man attempts to define his manhood by how many other men fear him or look up to him. This speaks to our desire for power and influence, and every man has an innate desire for it. And men will often pursue intimidation through almost any means: physically (I'm stronger, bigger, faster, and tougher), financially (I'm richer), professionally (I'm more influential), intellectually (I'm smarter), socially (I'm more important), relationally (I'm better looking, dress better, more sophisticated) and even spiritually (I'm a better person). Intimidation also shows itself as anger and control issues in our family when the people closest to us fear us the most (i.e., wife and children). Manhood is not defined by how many people fear you, but rather by how many people believe in you and trust you.

I don't know about you, but when it comes to being a man, I've had to learn the hard way

that true manhood is not measured by the number of degrees I have, the position I hold, the number of people who know me, or the size of my paycheck, but rather by God's opinion of me and serving others.

Chapter prayer points and meditation 

Get a quiet place and begin to pray for yourself with the below prayer points.

• Ou Lord! give me a new heart! a heart that aligns with your biblical definition of manhood. **Ezekiel 36:26** *"I will give you a new heart and put a new spirit within you; I will remove your heart of stone and give you a heart of flesh"*.

• Ou Lord! give me the grace to be the type of man you want me to be.

Psalm 143:10-12 *"10 teach me to do your will, for you are my God; may your good Spirit lead me on level ground. 11 For your name's sake, Lord, preserve my life; in your righteousness, bring me out of trouble".*

- Give me the wisdom that will allow me to function according to your purpose.

2 Chronicles 1:10 *"Now grant me wisdom and knowledge, so that I may lead this people. For who is able to govern this great people of Yours?"*

Chapter declaration

- I am the man that God says I am!
- I will never allow my financial status, my paycheck to dictate my manhood!
- Men are first servants therefore; I shall strive to serve my people in every possible way, starting with my family.

- I am the man my family needs!

- I am that man my nation needs!

- I am that man the world needs!

CHAPTER 3

Who is a man?

We live in a world that is demonically manipulated by demons of the air, land and water which have created other genders besides Males and Females. There is no such thing as other in the biblical definition of man.

Join me for a rediscovery of the man's purpose as it was meant to be.

What Is a Real Man?

Men Need a God-Given Identity if They Are to Fulfill Their True Purpose.

Let us critically analyze the following categories of males who consider themselves to be real men. After analyzing the below roles each male has described himself to be, you are expected to draw your conclusion of which man is authentic and which man is an imposter.

Man Number 1: "I am a Real Man because I complete the traditional role of a man. I support my family financially while my wife cares for the children and the home. As long as I provide a roof over their heads and food for them to eat, I am fulfilling my duty as a husband and a father".

Man number 2: Says, "I am the Real Man because I have a culturally progressive role, I share household and childrearing responsibilities with my wife while we both pursue careers".

Man number 3: Explains, "I am the Real Man because I have been freed from male stereotypes and have decided to take on the nurturer role of caring for the children and home while my wife goes to work".

Self-introspection Exercise

Write down the category you think portrays the qualities of a real man. In addition, explain why you think so.

____

____

____

____

____

These are some of the kinds of male qualities that are competing for men's acceptance today. Many men feel as if they 're being asked to guess what a real man is by determining which man has the most convincing facial expressions and answers. Yet there seems to be no clear-cut to it.

Society keeps mixing and matching these images until men don't know what's expected of them anymore. They are confused and frustrated as they try to sort through their expectations for manhood while feeling pressure from the various parts of society that are promoting these images or an impossible combination of them. Meanwhile, Hollywood is flooding society with intriguing icons of masculinity, such as James Bond and Rambo. Even though these images are superheroes rather than real men, it's sometimes hard to escape their allure. It's difficult not to start thinking that a real man should somehow imitate the power and resourcefulness they exhibit.

A Real Man, however, should be a man that is after God's Heart, that understand his call/purpose in society. A man that possess the six virtues explain by Apostle Paul in Chapter 2 in increasing measures.

Reflection: Which worldly expectations do I need to let go of to embrace true biblical manhood?

Chapter prayer points and meditation

Get a quiet place and begin to pray for yourself with the prayer points below.

- Man's True Identity

 Genesis 1:27 – I am created by God as a man with a divine purpose.

- Biblical Manhood

1 Corinthians 16:13-14 – I will stand firm in faith, be courageous, and lead with love. A

- Man After God's Heart

Acts 13:22 – I will seek God above all and follow him.

Chapter declaration

I am a man created in God's image, called to live with purpose, integrity, and responsibility. My identity is in Christ, not in the world's definitions of manhood.

CHAPTER 4

A problem with gender roles

The reality is that men have historically defined their manhood by their roles and the duties they carry out for their families and society, which is what makes our contemporary cultural environment unpleasant for us today. However, there has been a significant change in the roles that men and women play. The social norms are evolving. The past ten (10) years or so have seen this. We are going through a cultural shift, and conflicting views on masculinity are giving us males a lot of trouble. We are attempting to understand what it means to be a real man in the modern world while being pushed in numerous directions at once.

Today males are in a condition of crisis and internal struggle, according to the current literature on the changes in men's lives. Numerous studies have shown that **men are unsure about their identities and what women want from them.** Men are attempting to deal with the collision of modern cultural demands and conventional ideals of what a man should be, which they have internalized through family, society, or natural inclination, without having a clear sense of who they are.

Thus, fundamental ideas about what it means to be a man are being challenged. They sense a displacement. Either they are angry and trying to stop the change, or they are frustrated and trying to fit into a new but hazy idea of who they are.

Do we intend to completely renounce established traditional roles?

If so, what will take their place? Many guys have unanswered inquiries, including the following and I am sure you can relate:

1. Is a guy still expected to provide for his family and provide protection? The woman says she doesn't need a man's protection. A man is unsure about what he should do for a woman these days.

2. Does a guy still exercise authority and leadership in the home? This is no longer obvious. You don't have my authority, the woman asserts. I am not a servant. I choose how

I want to spend my money. I act as I please. I'll give you a call when I'm prepared for you. A man no longer understands how he should interact with his woman.

3. Is chivalry still appropriate for men? Should he pay for a woman's lunch on a date, accompany her, open doors for her, etc.? A woman will remark, "That's okay," when a male pulls out a chair for her. I appreciate your help, but I'll remove my chair. Sometimes a man will be insulted when a man opens a door for her. She'll retort, "Do you think I'm crippled?" A woman can look at a man strangely if he stands up in a room when she enters out of respect. A man is unsure about whether he should be polite to a woman.

4. Is a man still the protector of his home, possessions, and nation? Gun-toting women are becoming more prevalent in the military and law enforcement. Some males are unsure of how to respond to these modifications. When a woman enters the house wearing a uniform, her husband is frightened to greet her. He will get up and exclaim, "Sergeant!" She doesn't need me to protect her, many guys believe. Men are unsure about whether women still require them.

Is there anything that distinguishes men from women in modern society? That issue is challenging to answer in light of the aforementioned facts. The gender roles of men and women are shifting and becoming unclear.

So what must you do in the twenty-first century to be a man? Concerning women, who are men? How can men differentiate between the multiple definitions of masculinity that are marketed throughout the globe? You are not alone if you are a man and feel that your life is at work, in your relationships, and overall is being flipped upside down. Being a male nowadays is the most difficult thing in the world. All ages of men are struggling with conflicting ideas about what it means to be a guy. What really happened?

Not only were our parents from a different generation, but they also had distinct ideas about what it meant to be a man or a woman. Up until quite recently, historically speaking, roles that were expected of men and women didn't frequently overlap. Historic Positions there is a very regular pattern of roles for men and women that have existed for fifty, one hundred, five hundred, two thousand, and four thousand years. Roles for men and women were distinct and did not overlap recognized and esteemed.

This enduring pattern was motivated by several highly pragmatic factors. Although there have always been some exceptions to the rule across people and civilizations, most families have always behaved in the manner described below. Today's male-female relationships are still influenced by this conventional pattern. Gender roles were <u>Primarily Determined by Biology In premodern times</u>. Men often had greater physical strength than women, therefore they were the ones who went hunting and supporting the family. Females take care of the youngsters since they are naturally capable of bearing offspring. In general, a woman could not override Biology through the use of pharmaceutical processes to substitute A man.

A father didn't have to consider if it was his wife or it's him that would raise the kids at home. Because roles were set by biology, they were less difficult.

Living Day to Day Was a Battle for Survival. In addition, the physical environment in which people lived was more hostile, making daily life a challenge. Due to his physical superiority, the male naturally assumed the role of family provider and protector.

Making a living was a particularly precarious task at that time. The father had to essentially put his life in danger to provide for his family. Because of this, his wife and kids looked to him for guidance and appreciated his essential role in ensuring their survival. They were reliant on him. There was no assurance that a guy would return alive from going out to buy food for his family. He could suffer a deadly animal attack or perish from exposure. So when he returned home, the wife was delighted to see him. The Men had to take life-threatening risks to survive.

The same fundamental mindset prevailed in the era of our parents and grandparents when most husbands were the only breadwinners in their households and ladies stayed at home. The entire family celebrated the father's homecoming that evening. Why? He had been out there, trying to survive in a dangerous environment. It was sometimes difficult to find work. Working long hours in the fields or underground in a coal mine was occasionally the only job a guy could find. A man's wife knew he had risked his health or possibly his life to keep bread on the table when he returned home limping.

Before the time of your grandparents or perhaps your parents, each person was aware of their position and had the necessary abilities to fill it. The woman understood what she had to do, and she did it, just as the husband knew what he needed to do and did it. Because there was no ambiguity regarding gender roles, relationships were very simple even when surviving was challenging. No one had to question whether a man or a woman was trespassing on the other's property. She was responsible for taking care of the kids, cooking, and maintaining the house. To supply the family with food and a place to live, it was his responsibility to go hunting or gather crops.

Relationships were less difficult in this way because life was simple. A Natural Appreciation Was Created through Interdependence men and women were interdependent as a result of their survival cooperation, which led to a mutual appreciation. They respected one another because they each put forth a lot of effort and completed their respective tasks. It came with no effort on their part. Being extremely clear about and accepted for their respective responsibilities made it natural.

There wasn't always the traditional bond between husband and wife in these marriages. Simple desires like eating together, sex, having children, and safety drove the guy. He wasn't driven by chit-chat, sentimental interaction, or psychological or emotional sensitivity. To take care of his fundamental necessities, he returned home.

In most cases, a man's wife would revere and adore him because she understood he risked his life to care for her and the kids, not because he was a decent guy or an adoring companion. Because of everything he had done for her, she adored him. He wasn't an emotional, romantic guy, and that's why he didn't win her respect and affection. She appreciated his gift. She wouldn't respect him if he didn't endure the weather and return with fresh meat. The father admired and loved the lady for her commitment to the family, spending time caring for the kids, and making a home, not because she was attractive. He respected her because she was the mother of his children and because he saw the importance and value of the work she was performing. He wasn't concerned about who would take care of the kids' needs for food, cleaning, or garment washing. He was proud of his wife for doing all of that. This indicates that many of our early progenitors did not consider romance to be an important aspect of their lives. They were too preoccupied with trying to live. There isn't much time for sentiment when you're operating in survival mode.

The time for romance wasn't there in survival mode. Up until very recently, many married couples similarly experienced things. A guy worked all day long. He was focused on supporting and safeguarding his family. When he gets home, he does not have time for romance. He just has two desires: eating and sex. He wasn't worried about treating his wife to a meal out or about taking her shopping or about giving her money to spend. He needed his money just to get by. Simply put, the connection was one of survival and my responsibility to keep you safe. That is life: doing whatever it takes to get these things done. The guy viewed his marriage as a collaboration, but at the time, the definition of a partnership was different.

He didn't think his wife was as good as he was or on par with him. Instead, cooperation meant that he and she each had a role to perform. This idea of marriage was taught to both men and women. **Instead of recognizing the equality of**

men and women, a husband and wife appreciate each other for the unique contributions they each made to the union. This is where our society's origins lie and this is where I want to take every male of all ages reading this book.

Chapter prayer points and meditation

Prayer and Meditation:

1. Father, You created me with a purpose. Guide me to fulfill the role You have designed for me.

- Meditation: Proverbs 20:7 – "The righteous man walks in his integrity; his children are blessed after him."

2. Grant me wisdom to lead with integrity. Help me to be a man of self-control, faithfulness, and respect in my home and community.

- Meditation: 1 Timothy 3:2-3 – "Now the overseer is to be above reproach, faithful to his wife, temperate, self-controlled, respectable, hospitable, able to teach."

3. Teach and strengthen me to be a responsible steward over all that You have entrusted to me.

- Meditation: Genesis 2:15 – "The Lord God took the man and put him in the Garden of Eden to work it and take care of it."

4. Lord, order my steps and delight in my path as I walk in Your ways.

- Meditation: Psalm 37:23 – The steps of a good man are ordered by the Lord, and He delights in his way.

5. Help me to do justly, love mercy, and walk humbly with You.

- Meditation: Micah 6:8 – He has shown you, O man, what is good; and what does the Lord require of you but to do justly, to love mercy, and to walk humbly with your God?

Declaration:

I am a man created by God with a divine purpose. I will walk in obedience, lead with wisdom, and fulfill my calling as God intended.

CHAPTER 5

Contemporary Roles

Today's men and women have very different lives because they are not entirely dependent on one another for survival and protection. Both their roles and strategies have changed significantly. Men no longer work in the occupation that they have almost exclusively held for millennium. Men used to have specific roles that they did not share with their wives. How was masculinity assessed?

In the olden days, the advice to young men was, "Get a career, son, so you can support your family and be the head of the house." A man was assessed based on his ability to provide for his family and support himself. However, because of the shift that happened in society, these characteristics are no longer considered to be the primary markers of masculinity. This is because women have proven over the years to be able to do them and they are doing a good job so far. We have a lot of children being raised by single mothers. And Yes, we cannot blame the women for this, as their natural care and love for the family made her accept by default what was supposed to be a man's responsibility in the home. <u>My question is, where are the Men of this Generation?</u> Society is crying bitterly for man to be restored to their leadership role.

The traditional model, in which the woman stays at home to care for the children while her husband works, is still followed by a lot of couples, especially when the children are young. However, contemporary ideas about men's and women's roles in relationships often have a greater influence on these traditional marriage roles.

These days, with the prevalence of birth control and simultaneous employment, a husband and wife may choose not to have children. It's commonly believed that women are only responsible for reproduction, and a woman will often tell a man if and when she plans to have children. This is not always the case however, even if they do have a child, the woman will stay at home with the child all day, every day. Daycare and other childcare options allow her to work outside the home, either part-time or full-time. This change has resulted in additional stress for the family. Studies by researchers like Claire Hughes and Susan Golombok, such as those cited in "The Psychological Effects of Early Social Deprivation" (2010), have observed instances where children who spend significant time with nannies or daycare workers may not immediately recognize or have a strong bond with their parents. These findings align with attachment theory, notably the work of John Bowlby, which emphasizes the crucial role of primary caregivers in shaping children's social and emotional development.

In addition, the kids' nanny might be teaching them anything while the parents are at work.

This means that the parents don't know who is raising their kids. Furthermore, a man now needs to find another way to show his wife appreciation because, in the past, a woman's respect for her husband came from her ability to bear and raise children. Owing to the established pattern, when a wife asks for respect from him, he might occasionally respond, "Well, what are you doing to earn it?" In the twenty-first century, relationships can be difficult. Our current state is not one of survival. Safety and survival are not as important to most of us as they once used to be.

What can a man offer a woman today that women cannot provide for themselves?

Have you ever wondered why there are so many divorces in today's world? One explanation is that women might now tell men up front, "I'm leaving if you can't handle this properly." My grandmother is the mother of 8 children. When she was struggling, she was unable to tell my grandfather, "I'm going to leave you." To where was she going? She had not received any professional or academic training, nor had she been prepared for work outside the home. She lived at home all her life.

Men are still getting used to the shift, and for women, independence is still a relatively new position. The traditional male roles of protector and provider have been largely supplanted by women. She has a handbag containing a revolver, mace, and a cell phone so she can call the police immediately. Then, what does the man do? In response to his assertion that he is her protector, she says, "I don't need you to protect me." The world has changed since Men no longer recognize their responsibilities to women.

In contemporary society, with evolving gender roles and increased opportunities for women in various domains, the question of what men can offer women that women cannot provide for themselves has become a topic of discussion. This question touches upon the shifting dynamics of relationships, roles, and expectations between men and women. While there is no one-size-fits-all answer, several perspectives shed light on this complex issue.

Biblical insights provide one perspective on the roles and contributions of men and women in relationships. For example, Ephesians 5:25 states, ***"Husbands, love your wives, just as Christ***

loved the church and gave himself up for her." This verse emphasizes sacrificial love and selflessness as essential qualities that men can offer women in relationships. It suggests that men have a unique role in providing emotional support, protection, and leadership within the context of a partnership or marriage.

Additionally, biblical teachings often emphasize the importance of mutual respect, communication, and partnership between men and women. Proverbs 31 describes the virtuous woman who is industrious, resourceful, and wise, highlighting women's capabilities and contributions outside traditional gender roles. This perspective underscores the idea that both men and women have valuable qualities and strengths to offer in relationships, and their contributions complement each other.

In contemporary society, men can offer women various forms of support, companionship, and partnership that go beyond traditional gender roles. Emotional support, empathy, and understanding are qualities that men can provide in relationships, fostering trust, intimacy, and mutual respect. Men can also offer women companionship, shared experiences, and a sense of belonging, enriching their lives through meaningful connections and shared memories.

Furthermore, men can contribute to women's personal and professional growth by encouraging their ambitions, nurturing their talents, and providing development opportunities. In a rapidly changing world, where women are increasingly pursuing education, careers, and leadership roles, men can play a supportive role in helping women achieve their goals and aspirations.

Ultimately, the question of what men can offer women today that women cannot provide for themselves is multifaceted and subjective. While women are capable of self-sufficiency and independence in many aspects of life, meaningful relationships are built on mutual respect, love, and partnership, where both men and women contribute their unique strengths and qualities to create fulfilling and enriching connections.

In Ephesians 5:23,it states: ***"For the husband is the head of the wife as Christ is the head of*** *the church, his body, of which he is the Savior."* Similarly, in Colossians 3:18-19, it says: ***"Wives, submit yourselves to your husbands, as is fitting in the Lord. Husbands, love your wives and do not be harsh with them.*** "The Bible doesn't explicitly state why women need men, but it does provide principles and insights into the roles and relationships between men and women. One perspective often cited is from Genesis 2:18, where God says:

"It is not good for the man to be alone. I will make a helper suitable for him."

This verse is often interpreted as highlighting the complementary nature of men and women in relationships. It suggests that God created woman to be a companion and helper for man, indicating a mutual dependence and partnership between the sexes. While this verse specifically addresses the creation of Eve as a companion for Adam, it underscores the broader idea that relationships between men and women are intended to be supportive, nurturing, and mutually beneficial.

Additionally, throughout the Bible, there are numerous examples of men and women working together, supporting each other, and building meaningful relationships. From the partnership of Adam and Eve in Genesis to the collaboration of Paul and Phoebe in the New Testament, the Bible portrays men and women as equal partners in God's kingdom, each contributing their unique gifts and abilities to fulfill God's purposes.

Ultimately, while the Bible doesn't explicitly state why women need men, it emphasizes the importance of mutual respect, love, and partnership in relationships between men and women. Both men and women are valued and essential in God's eyes, and their relationships are intended to reflect God's love and grace in the world.

Evolving Roles and Shared Responsibilities

There once existed worlds apart for men and women. Man's world meant work and survival. For a woman, her children and home were her entire world. Role divisions were evident. They knew exactly where they wanted to end up. A woman's departure from home to attend work signifies that she is no longer the primary caregiver for the house. The man and the woman don't know what their responsibilities are in the house. They don't understand. Your wife now also brings home the pig, whereas before it was your father who would bring home the bacon. Other than that, she had two pigs before you were married.

She has bacon; she doesn't need any more from you. **Who is the provider if both the husband and the wife are now bringing the bacon home?** <u>For men, that is a difficult question.</u> If both are making mortgage payments, then who is who?

<u>Today, Women are bringing home not only the bacon but also the pig!</u>

Your father was considered the owner of his house because he bought and paid for it. The man is no longer the owner of the house. The woman and the man have a right to it. Some men think back to the time when their fathers were the "man of the house." Currently, a woman will follow a man's lead if he puts his foot down. Men were taught concepts that are no longer relevant. Your father says to put her in her place. You say, but she owns the space. Point out to her which family member wears the pants, but she wears them too!

Many couples face difficult financial situations that require them to both work outside the home to make ends meet. The societal tendency for women to delay marriage, pursue careers, and enroll in college has had a significant impact on family life. Saying to his wife, "Honey, you have to raise the children," for example, would be met with her reply, "No, I'm going to work." Why? Because I want to use my knowledge and support a certain lifestyle that requires double pay, I'm going to work. But he wonders, who will raise the kids? It is you who bears and nurtures the child. She answers.

My company owns and operates a daycare center. I'm going to accept the job. What must a man do when his spouse makes more money than he does? Even though he believes he should take care of the household and provide for the family? He is both irritated and ashamed. This is one of the main causes of the frequent arguments in our contemporary relationships. Who is responsible for what gets us into constant arguments? Our perspectives and our customary responsibilities have been profoundly impacted by these and similar circumstances. What a man is has become meaningless to the female.

This development has caused anxiety in both men and women. For example, a woman may feel very guilty when she declares, "I'm a homemaker." Do you think that in the days of your parents or grandparents, people used to ask women, "So, what do you do?" It was never brought up. But these days, almost every woman is asked about her employment.

To state it differently, know what she stays away from doing. She does more than just raise her children at home, which suggests that she ought to feel guilty about it. It used to be so much easier for the woman who took care of her kids at home. Since every woman in the neighborhood was at home, she had help with her work. These days, a woman's homemaking is seen as an indication that something is wrong with her. They inquire, "What's wrong with her?" among other things. She must be lazy, lack creativity, not have enough education to pursue a career, need to start a family, etc. In society, there is a stereotype that "only dumb women stay at home."

The effects of changing gender roles can be upsetting to men and women equally. People are not sure how to act in this unfamiliar setting. It has become a psychological puzzle for many. Many people are feeling tight and confused, and they are wondering what's wrong with them. Right away, I'll tell you what's wrong: it's simply a different planet. Independence Has Changed the Limits of Appreciation. Women in the modern era are growing more self-reliant and independent, and they no longer feel that men are necessary to look out for and provide for them. Men struggle with this. They're all trying to get along in their relationships, but they're not sure who is responsible for what.

A man might ask women, "Are you going to pay for yours?" when they are out to lunch, for example. Thirty years ago, the man made an automated payment. How come? It was man's duty to provide. But these days, when a man takes a woman out to dinner and finds he doesn't have enough cash, she reaches into her purse and assures him she'll pay the difference. He feels degraded, but she is not embarrassed because she has the money. She still thinks well of him. Because she feels that there aren't many good guys in the world, she likes him. Women's traditional value of men is being undermined by their increasing independence on one hand. But also, again Why is the Men not having enough money to pay for both their dinner plates? Why is he earning less? What happened to the men working hard to earn more than the women? Men need to rise again and stand up as authority bearers, Man Must Work and Earn More so that he is not intimidated by Women. It is not the woman's fault that she earns a lot.

Despite coughing up TB in the winter's bitter cold and precipitation, to provide for the family. The family relied solely on them to survive. It was the reason why women loved them. Sometimes a woman will say, "I can't do that," in response to someone asking her why she wouldn't leave her abusive husband after disclosing that he is abusing her. What a considerate reply. Some things about him appeal to her. What would you think of a man who put his life in anger every day to protect you, and the kids, and to make ends meet?

You will think highly of him because you know what he is going through to support the family. Because of this, even though your father didn't always act honorably, your mother's love and respect for him came naturally. He meant a lot to her. However, this isn't always the case these days. "Let me be clear up front: if you can't cut the mustard, you can leave whenever you're ready," a woman can say to a man who seems interested. In addition, if we get married, I want you to sign a prenuptial agreement so that anything I contribute to the marriage will be mine in the event of a divorce. The bible commends a man to love and the wife to submit. Perhaps man do not know what it is to love women so that the women don't have to tell them leave.

Women no longer appreciate men in the same manner that they formerly did since they are now able to meet their wants. Because they believe their women don't require them, some husbands are terrified of their spouses. The fact that for the first time recorded in history, men and women seek one another more for love and friendship than for survival and protection is another fundamental development. As a species, we no longer prioritize the same things. In their relationships, people seek something more.

To be content, I require attention. My father was not able to go out for dinner with my mother or take her on walks. There wasn't enough time for it. He made my mother happy just by making sure the family had access to clothing, running water, and other necessities

What can men do these days to win women over? That's the challenge. Has a man ever questioned what a woman desires before? In the past, husbands would inquire, "Woman, what else do you need from me?" to their wives. I gave you a roof over your head and food in the kitchen.

Deepening Emotional and Relational Bonds

Effective communication, intimacy, and sensitivity were not concerns when the man gave his life to support his spouse and family. A man has no time to learn how to be a good man with ladies. Again, he was tired, he needed food and sex, and when he came home, it was dark. The rationale was that he owed the house and the food, and it was time to make amends. But today's women want intimacy and interaction. "Talk to me." Have you shown me any love during the day?

The social context has changed, so we have more time to think about these concerns. Women used to say things like, "Don't touch me right now! I'm on my period and I don't have the right hormone balance. A man now needs to find out what kind of "mood" his wife is in. There wasn't time for the caveman to check his wife's attire. You know the role and strength of men, therefore you're not thinking in terms of feelings. It was a new way of life, but not always a better one. Men are still developing their ability to communicate and be intimate in relationships. A woman may wonder why her partner finds it so hard to talk to her. He can't think of anything to say, and she doesn't know his predicament. Let's say, for example, that he works in a lower-paying position while she has a terrific career in leadership or administration.

What topics do they talk about? Since it is not required of him to do so to keep his job, he is not yet communicating at her level of complexity. After that, she says a few words, and he starts to become scared. He says to himself, Oh, that's a big phrase. His status as a leader seems to have eroded, leaving him confused of what to do. During this challenging time for our nation, women need to understand the men in their lives. Imagine that when a woman marries a men and they move in together, she urges him to "be a man." He asserts.

Wives use to be kind and patient with their husbands. In today's environment, relationships also demand passion. Remember how a man used to question a woman, "Woman, are you ready or not?" in the past? No captivating introductions were given. He would say. All set, sweetheart! Now go ahead and bring it on. It was there. However, modern women demand that their husbands turn down the lights, light scented candles, and arrange flowers around the room. What's happening, the men inquire. Guys, you have to work for it now.

It requires work! Nowadays, women expect men to start showing them affection in the morning, giving them breakfast, taking them to lunch, running the bath water, making five calls to confess their feelings, picking them up in a limousine, and taking them out to a fancy dinner, all in the hopes of rewarding them that evening. They won't get paid until they put in the work, however there's no guarantee.

Today, it costs a lot of money to win over our women. Don't give up though—this is just another way to hydrate your blossom. **1 Peter 3:7** *"Likewise, husbands, live with your wives in an understanding way, showing honor to the woman as the weaker vessel, since they are heirs with you of the grace of life, so that your prayers may not be hindered"*.

1. What can man provide women today that women are not able to provide for themselves?

____

____

____

____

____

____

____

____

____

____

____

____

2. What can women do for men today that men are not able to do for themselves?

____

____

____

____

____

____

____

____

____

____

____

____

____

____

3. Is it good for women to stay without a man?

____

____

____

____

____

____

____

____

____

____

____

____

CHAPTER 6

Roles versus Purpose

Everything ultimately boils down to how men define themselves and their worth. Because men like to link their identities with their duties, they frequently lose their sense of self when their obligations shift. Anything they decide to replace their archaic notion of what it means to be a man could never be a real or satisfying role for them. Even worse, men who are unsure about their position in the world either reject it or abuse it—for example, by misusing their power to beat or abuse women. We have increased cases of gender-based violence due to man not using their God-given strength correctly. This is a result of frustration, but the problem is man punches the wrong person (the woman). They should punch themselves because it is they who are failing the women and society.

The question now arises, What are the actions that men should take to regain authority over their identity and course of action?

The answer is found in the book of Romans 12: 2

"Do not conform to the pattern of this world but be transformed by the renewing of your mind. Then you will be able to test and approve what God's will is—his good, pleasing and perfect will".

Man needs to stop complying with what the current society has labeled them to be. That is a stereotype that is not true and needs to be rebuked. Man must begin with an entirely new way of thinking. They must renew their mind by first accepting Jesus as the Chief Director of their lives and home. Only then can man be able to know their purpose in God, which is a pleasing, and perfect will of God for them.

Men need to understand that there is more to life than just following social norms. A man's goal should define his position and behavior, not the other way around. This suggests that comprehending the fundamental purpose of man, rather than just adapting to the changing times, is the answer to the male conundrum, even though some adaptation to the times will be necessary.

Man needs to focus more on God and stop focusing on roles. A man ought to think about objectives, their purpose in God, in the home, and society. Man for years, have been misjudging their own values, and this is why they are currently experiencing issues. For years the identity and purpose of a man have never truly been determined by their roles. Even while roles might have benefits or drawbacks, they ultimately just serve to illustrate customs and culture. This is wrong though.

We cannot learn what it is to be a true man by studying the society in which we now reside (Man must not conform to the pattern set up by society). Men must possess a self-awareness that is unaffected by social norms or the opinions of others (renewal of the mind should take place in every man and boy child). This can be achieved if every man can be honest to themselves and read what James 1:15 says.

"If any of you lacks wisdom, let him ask God, who gives generously to all without reproach, and it will be given him," is the authoritative source".

Every man must ask wisdom from God on how to be and become the man God created to be a leader and rule over all things, not forgetting that together with the women they are both co-heirs to the kingdom of God. Man needs to cultivate a habit of having a relationship with God. Men must start going to church, the fact that we see more women in church is also not very correct. Man must begin to seek God, they must come off their high horses and come to the feet of the Lord Jesus to seek counsel and wisdom. In this manner, man can become the leader God created. A man should further invest time in prayer. Prayer is not a women's thing as many people think so. Prayer is for everyone, both man and women.

Luke 18: 1 *"And he spoke a parable unto them to this end, that men ought always to pray, and not to faint. Meaning all men must pray, male and female"*.

I challenge every man and boy child to start praying for wisdom to become a man who is directed by God. A practice to Become a Godly defined man as presented by **Sternberg and**

Gluck, 2019 and seeking God's wisdom through prayers. Exercise the following:

1. Have an open mind. It is believed that openness is a characteristic of knowledgeable people. Being open-minded means considering all available options before accepting information that contradicts our preconceived notions or past experiences. Curiosity, inventiveness, intelligence, and interest in various viewpoints are all indicators of being open to new experiences. Relying solely on our existing knowledge might impede our capacity for broader thinking.

2. Have Compassion. Perceptive individuals can recognize the perspectives of others. They care deeply for the well-being of others and the well-being of all people.

3. Do self-introspection. Understanding oneself is a crucial component of knowledge and personal development. To grow from experience, highly reflective people are able and willing to critically examine their own beliefs and actions. They do this without becoming defensive. As knowledge grows, reflection aids people in understanding what they know and don't know.

4. Have a methodical approach. A wise person knows how to strike a balance between their interests and those of others to achieve the greater good. A prudent judgment will take into consideration a variety of interests and work toward achieving the common good.

5. Deal with uncertainty. Very wise people have learned from experience how uncertain and uncontrollable life is. They have learned to trust in their strengths to cope with whatever comes their way.

6. Wisdom of old age. As people grow older, they become less self-centered and more connected to others and the world in general. As we become more conscious of death, we reevaluate what is truly important in life and realize that external sources of self-worth, such as fame and money, are less valuable than our essential pursuits.

7. Wisdom comes from overcoming crises. When smart people face crises and obstacles in life, they can apply valuable life lessons learned from past experiences of overcoming adversity.

8. Look at the big picture. A wise person is not primarily guided by immediate goals of action, but rather by the ultimate goal of his life as a whole. Having a broader perspective makes it easier to put aside complex details and focus on what seems most important.

9. Purpose. A sense of direction and purpose (goals that are meaningful to oneself and others) greatly contributes to the development of wisdom. Meaning in life is related to emotional stability and resilience during vulnerable and stressful life events.

10. Regulation of emotions. Emotional stability is a necessary element of wisdom. Emotion regulation is the ability to regulate emotions in ways that help achieve short- and long-term goals (for example, when faced with emotionally charged events). For example, humor can be used to strengthen emotional bonds with others or suppress negative emotions.

In summary, as a man you need wisdom that provides inner resources to cope with adversity and difficulties. Wisdom enables individuals to adapt to life situations through a thorough understanding and acceptance of themselves, others, and the world.

Understanding your Role and Purpose as a Man

Men must consequently have a God-given identity to serve their real calling. We need to understand what God's original plans were for them. We need to revisit the Creator's original design for both men and women. To accomplish this we must remember once more that when men are unaware of who they are, it negatively affects not only their callings and satisfaction but also the fulfillment of their families and the entire society.

God has endowed men with a special leadership impact, which explains this. The family, society, and the globe depend on how well the man does. If we do not solve the male identity dilemma, I think our generation as a whole is in jeopardy. This reality cannot be denied. Therefore, the solution for man and boy child of the current and upcoming generation is to:

- Discover God's plan for their lives.
- Emphasize God's plan rather than social norms.
- Living in alignment with the true essence in God.

- Growing in the Fear of God and Respect for humanity.

- Cultivate a life of humility, servanthood, and sacrifice, following the example of Christ.

- Embrace godliness and righteousness, pursuing a life of integrity, love, and steadfast faith.

Men are free to realize their potential and destiny if they understand the roles and responsibilities God has given them and the true nature of their union with women.

They can fulfill their potential as men despite the contradictory messages society currently sends, as men we have to be sure of who we are and where we belong in the world. Rediscovering God's purpose for men and women will give you a new sense of purpose and direction. With this knowledge, men can realize and achieve more than they ever thought possible, and women can value men in new ways while helping them follow their mission.

What does it mean to be a "real man"?

The first step in gaining this knowledge is understanding the significance of God's intentional creation.

Chapter review 

1. Traditionally, men have used their responsibilities to define what it means to be a man.

2. Men and women have historically played different, non-overlapping roles.

3. Relationships between men and women are different because we are no longer

dependent on each other for safety and livelihood.

4. Men experience a crisis of identity and meaning.

5. Human life can be destroyed by neglect and confusion about man's purpose (The Rise of Gays in Society).

6. If a person bases their identity on their job, they lose their identity when the job is taken away, creating an identity crisis.

7. A person's purpose defines who he is, not his responsibility.

8. Fundamental human motivations transcend society and customs.

9. If we observe the chaotic society around us, we will never understand what it means to be a real human being.

10. The purpose of things is found only in the mind of the Creator.

11. For humans to achieve their ultimate goals, they must have an identity that comes from God.

12. People's mission and happiness are undermined when they do not recognize the true nature of not only themselves, but also their families and society as a whole because this man's actions affect his family, society, and the entire planet.

13. A true human being accepts himself as he is and lives according to God's creation intention.

CHAPTER 7

Purpose of Men

Timothy 3:4-5 says that **"God designed men to lead"**, and they are encouraged to lead well.

As you read this chapter, ask the Holy Spirit to show you areas of your life that you can improve upon to become that man, husband, and father that your family needs you to be.

1. To build and establish a Relationship with God

God designed you for a specific purpose. God created everything, but he realized something was missing. The Bible says repeatedly in Genesis 1, ***"God saw that it was good,"*** but only when God created man did the Bible say in verse 31, ***"God saw that it was good." He saw all that he had made, and it was very good."*** When God created Adam, he did not abandon him. Instead, he spoke to him, blessed him, gave him challenges, and encouraged him to enjoy the land and all that God had provided for him.

In Genesis 3: 8, Adam and Eve heard God walking in the garden in the afternoon. We know God is looking for them because God calls out to them, "Where are you?" You were forced to live in a fallen world, the same world you and I live in today. However, that does not mean God has stopped loving them. The Lord initially told them that eating the fruit of the tree would mean death, but He saved their lives. God still wants to speak to them and their children, and He always wants to hear from you. **If you want to reach your full potential as the man God has called you to, you have to set aside time daily to commune with God. This means to talk to God in prayer, reading his word and worshiping him daily.**

We cannot put our relationship with God aside and resume it only when it is convenient. When you do this, you are doing yourself a disservice by closing your ears to your ability to fully tune into what God is trying to communicate to you. **God always speaks the question is, "Do you always listen to him?** Do you hear his voice when he speaks?

2. Financial Provider

Before God blessed Adam with a wife, he was blessed with a job Genesis 2: 15 says, ***"The Lord God took the man and put him in the Garden of Eden to work and take care of him."*** There is a reversal of roles in many families today. The wife plays the role of head of the household. THERE IS NOTHING WRONG WITH WOMEN HAVING JOBS, BUT THEY SHOULD NOT ALWAYS BE UNDER PRESSURE TO JUST MEET THE NEEDS OF THEIR FAMILIES BECAUSE IT IS THE RESPONSIBILITY OF THE HUSBAND. However, a successful marriage is one in which the husband and wife feel equally responsible for providing for themselves. Remember that Eve was created because Adam could not find a suitable helper (Genesis 2: 20)

Neither party should feel taken advantage of nor should they feel like what they do for the family goes unnoticed. There will be unexpected times in life when the husband or wife may have to carry the financial burden more than the other does. This does not mean that one partner should have to cover up for the lack of the other that is just how life is and should be understood as such.

As someone who advocates for the needs of families, that does not just mean taking home a paycheck. This will ensure that you are making financial decisions that benefit your family rather than harm them. Spending money to satisfy addictions of all kinds i.e. gambling, alcohol, drugs, and sex, costs families financially. A real man invests in his family before he takes care of his social life.

Those addicted to pornography may not have spent money to feed their addiction, but there is always a cost to pay. They pay the price they cannot see, which is their Destiny and time. The enemy keeps them in pornography and blinds them to their real identities and purpose in life. The enemy always takes something, even when you cannot see it. Spiritually he is taking a lot from you when you indulge in acts that cause addiction. Addictions mean you have a legal contract with the enemy, and you cannot get out of the contract until he has destroyed you completely. Fellow man be warned. Seek your freedom from addiction by surrendering all to Jesus and he will strengthen you and defeat the enemy for you.

3. A man needs to be the Spiritual Leader at home

It is the role of men to lead their homes spiritually. Youngsters are more directed by their visual sense than by their auditory sense. Furthermore, children turn to their fathers, grandfathers, older brothers, and other father figures for guidance. The priorities they saw in their family structure as children would reflect their priorities as adults.

Youngsters are naturally able to discern between sincere and false behavior. Whether you attend church religiously out of necessity, skip church, or pursue Christ with all of your heart, your children will know.

Your family will reap great benefits when you, as a man, decide to give your life to Christ. Being a faith-based leader is the easiest thing in the world. It is also the best way to lead a home that is directed by God.

4. As a functional man, leaving a Legacy worth Remembering is the way forward

The expectation to always be in control is something most men grapple with. They struggle with friendships, and many report that they do not have a close, trusted male friend who knows everything about them.

As Men, we, are commonly raised to believe that showing emotion indicates weakness. We feel the only way is to bottle our fears, doubts, trauma, disappointments, and failures up within ourselves. Many men may find it difficult to connect with their emotions, reflect on past wounds, or discuss traumatic experiences.

However, holding everything in is not a healthy approach. The healthy approach is to acknowledge and express emotions through self-reflection, open communication, seeking professional help, building emotional resilience, and creating a supportive community.

End of chapter quote

NB! There is still hope for you to find your way back to the man whom God created you to be, just pray and ask him to be in the driver's seat of your life.

"Your family will follow what you do, not what you say"

....

End of chapter questions

1. How does your current relationship with God reflect in your leadership as a man, husband, or father?

- Are you actively making time to commune with Him daily, or are you only seeking Him in times of crisis?

2. In what ways do your financial decisions impact your family's well-being and spiritual growth?

- Are you investing in your family's future, or are certain habits, addictions, or distractions holding you back from being a responsible provider?

3. What kind of spiritual legacy are you building for those who look up to you?

- If your children or younger men around you were to imitate your faith and lifestyle, would they be led closer to God or further away?

CHAPTER 8

Boy Child Upbringing

Proverbs 22:6 *"Train up a child in the way he should go; even when he is old he will not depart from it."*

Do not accept the child's behavior but rather raise the child's behavior in the biblical manner accepted and pleasing before God.

The Bible does not say to accept the children's character and behavior, as they grow, No! It says TRAIN THEM. As a parent, you need to train the children by mentoring and ushering them into what you want them to be. Most of the time, the boy children are brought up in a female-dominated home. The only example they receive is from the female figure. At school the teachers are females at home the child is only surrounded by lipsticks and Brazilian wigs. That environment automatically grooms the child **into a certain individual**. It's important to mind what games your son is playing, who stays with your son at home, what sport your son plays at school what pictures dominate your child's search engine, and who are your son's friends.

It is those small things that contribute to the mentoring of your child.

Mentoring is an automatic process. Everyday situations and the environment contribute to your child's development without you knowing.

We live in an error where children are protected by the government. However, you need to discipline your child otherwise you will raise an individual that is fit only for the streets (foolish child).

Proverbs 22:15 – *"Foolishness is bound in the heart of a child, but the rod of correction shall drive it far from him."* The children act and think very stupid at times, when you as a parent with the experience of life need to discipline your child. It is biblical to raise a rod to a child, for discipline, as this will deliver his life from foolishness. Moreover, the boy child cannot be raised in the same manner, as the girl child. The two are different and there should be certain strategies that should be part of the boy child upraising that are not in the girls upraising.

Proverbs 23: 13-14 *"Withhold not correction from the child for if thou beats him with the rod, he shall not die. 14 Thou shalt beat him with the rod, and shalt deliver his soul from hell."*

Challenges faced by boys in teenage hood

Body Image Issues

As teens grow from infancy to maturity, they may struggle to accept and feel comfortable with their bodies as they alter shape and size. After the heavenly child have vanished, they look in the mirror and see a weird man: lanky, spindly, hairy, and small.

I observe many young individuals striving to fit in and hoping that their classmates will accept them for who they are. They are currently experiencing a great deal of concern and anxiety as they prepare to execute one of the most significant jobs of their lives. When young people are taught that they do not belong or fit in, they may feel lonely, alienated, and miserable.

Television shows intended for this age, promote aggressive and violent conduct, rule-breaking, premarital sex, bullying, and other undesirable habits. This are the behaviors that are regarded as cool and will allow the boy child to fit in the society, while in actual fact they are bad and destroying characters in the long term. These behaviors should be discouraged from the home toward the boy child. Parents should learn to observe the boy child behavior more so that they can raise the rod to the boy at the appropriate time before it is too late.

Let us look at my example. I was educated to cherish moral and biblical concepts like honesty and integrity while being courteous, kind, compassionate, and forgiving. However, society claims that this belief is out of date or that it is a female-specific tendency. My pals rejected me for portraying these behaviors. If I was easily swayed by peer pressure, I may have tried to fit in and do what everyone else was doing. This could have resulted in me going out of the way that God have already paved for me. I want to encourage a boy child who feels alone and is bullied because he portrays the correct behavior which is rejected by society. I say to you, Be Confident, Have Courage, and Face the world knowing that you are correct and God accept your behavior first to yourself and you will stand being in the honesty, integrity, and in the fear of God.

Peer pressure is mostly responsible for our boy child's lack of sense of belonging. That is why children should be raised in a manner that pleases God. Teach your son to fear God more than man. Matthew 10:28 (Do not fear those who can murder the body but not the soul). Instead, dread him, who may destroy both spirit and body in hell. I therefore call on all fathers to be present for their boy child and be involved in their lives. As a man refuse to let the women raise your boy child alone. Fathers should be present at home and showcase to the boy child real-life examples of how a man should be in the home. Fathers, teach the boy child to pray, teach him to read the bible, and stimulate in him a habit of fellowshipping with God. In this manner, you have not only his present but also his soul from destruction and future.

Managing Your Time Stress

As the boy child advances in years, so does stress toward him. I.e. there is more pressure from school as you advance in greater grades. This inflicts stress on the child that is already struggling to find their identity and purpose in society. Activities such as dating, clubbing, and hanging out with friends provide a fresh and appealing social perspective that relief their stress. This is accepted by society, but it is wrong. When children are under emotional stress due to school or peer pressure from friends. The children should be able to talk to their parents, especially to their fathers to show them and advise them how to navigate the way through.

Society, these days, have succeeded in letting the children to raise themselves because all the parents are career oriented and are pushing for promotion to the next level in their careers. As such the boy child turns to drugs, alcohol, and everything that the streets present to him. I urge all parents to make time for their children and ask them of their struggles and direct them in the right way they should go. Let's be present parents.

The correct navigation though peer pressure and stress, can only be obtained through prayer and surrendering once self to Jesus. This is however possible if the Priest of the house has taken up his task to be the spiritual leader in his home.

Teens face a lot of pressure as they learn how to juggle all these demands. Suddenly teenagers are expected to act like adults. They need to independently manage their workload, draw, and implement sound conclusions, and manage their financial situation.

No matter how intelligent your son sounds, he needs guidance. Teenagers go through a lot of traumas. They are dealing with so many things and trying to find themselves in this confusing world. I advise you as a parent to be present always. Taking time off your busy schedule and talking to your son about the puberty stage and hormonal change, making fun of the situation, and getting your son's trust as early as possible will help him open up to you. As your child enters puberty, you need to have quadruple roles in his life. As the father, best friend, role model, and counselor as well.

Parental and Social Pressure

Parents often expect their children to achieve everything they want; when in reality they have the means to do so. Teens are under tremendous pressure to do well in school, make good friends, succeed in extracurricular activities, and be responsible for themselves and sometimes their younger siblings. Additionally, there is peer pressure. Teens are under pressure to conform to the current societal norms which is their wrong desires mostly, behavior, and appearance to be accepted and "popularity to their classmates.

Pressure increases when adolescents feel that everyone around them is trying to change.

Parents, teachers, parents, grandparents, siblings, friends, classmates, and social organizations all influence teenagers and pull them in different directions.

Issues with Physical and Mental Health

The following factors affect the health of teenagers:

Improper eating habits.

Teenagers' eating habits are below average and go unreported. They develop eating disorders and starve themselves or eat too much unhealthy, fatty, high-calorie junk food. They are not getting enough sleep. Teenagers give up sleep to do something and become someone.

According to the National Sleep Foundation, healthy adults need between 7 and 9 hours of sleep per night. The recommended sleeping time varies according to age (Brandon Peters, 2023):

- Newborns (0 to 3 months): Should average 14 to 17 hours of sleep a day, including naps.
- Infants (4 to 11 months): Should average 12 to 15 hours of sleep per day, including naps.
- Toddlers (12 to 35 months): Should average 11 to 14 hours, including naps.
- Preschoolers (3 to 5 years): Should average 10 to 13 hours per day.
- School-age children (6 to 13 years): Should average 9 to 11 hours per day.
- Teenagers (14 to 17 years): Should average 9 to 10 hours per day.

- Younger adults (18 to 25 years old): Should average 7 to 9 hours per day.
- Adults (26 to 64): Should average 7 to 9 hours per day.
- Older adults (age 65 and over): Should average 7 to 8 hours per day.

This shows that we are in the red every day. Both anxiety and depression. Teens are under a lot of mental stress due to hormonal fluctuations, confusion, and the stress of juggling schedules, setting priorities, achieving success, and meeting expectations. This manifests as irritability, hostility, sadness, anxiety, and sometimes complete weakness.

Lack of Heroes and Good Role Models

The meanest tyrants, the richest and spoiled brats, and the most destructive young men are often considered the most admired and popular. These individuals are glorified by the media, and their depravity is glorified in music, sports, movies, and other media.

Today our children are looking up to people that they have considered to be their role models, which are mainly identified from whatever media present to them. Everywhere the children go, they pick up on the corrupt morals of the "heroes" they see in the media. However, this only happens when the father is absent in the child's life. However, when the father is present in the life of the boy child, he can always compare the outside inspiration to the father's teachings and upbringing. The father becomes his role model, and he will strive to become just like the father.

Being a provider of the household, paying bills, and giving your child pocket money does not make you a present father! You need to be there physically, spiritually, and emotionally for your boychild.

In most cases, I Blame fathers for the increase of homosexuality in this present generation. They are forever absent in the lives of their children leaving their boys in the hands of women as the only inspiration. Yet they want to come and condemn the damage they caused. For society to thrive in the right direction, we need to be present in our son's lives. Fathers must be present and stop running away from their children.

I therefore put up a resistance, in this era, I urge men to renew their mind and begin to focus their attention away from destructive habitants such as alcohol, clubbing and drinking buddies. I challenge you, man, to read this book to divert your focus back to your children and family at large. I urge you to stand up and take up your place in your home. Remember that your first test of leadership is at the household level, you can't lead a society if you are failing to lead your home.

As I was researching on this book, I visited many schools. Picked a few samples of learners. In Grade 1. I picked boys who played with baby toys in the class and in grade 7 those boys that only hang out with girls. In my findings I recorded that all those kids have absent fathers in the families, either the boy is being taken

care of by the single mother, or big sister, or he is the only boy amongst 3 to 4 girls in the house.

Alcohol and drugs

You as a father, you cannot tell your son not to drink or smoke while you cannot live without the two. It is psychologically proven that even at a very young age, children imitate their parents' behavior. Parent and caregiver behavior presents powerful lessons to a child and leaves impressions on the developing mind. Children store in their minds both positive and negative images that may be imitated or tested at a later time (Eliza Martinez, 20218). Whatever the children see the parents doing, they later on go and do it in life.

I watched a movie once on television, it tells a story of how 2 boys saw the father abusing their mother, and drinking alcohol every day. As a matter of fact, he will send his sons to buy him beer, when he has his full, he will abuse the wife and the children saw all this happening, year in year out. One boy was sympathy with the mother and will keep on telling the mother to get a divorce, the other boy never really minded what was happening at his mother as he will secretly sip in his father beer or alcohol.

Often the boy child's first alcohol sip was taken at home from his parents' drink. I am sure you can guess what type of adult boys these 2 boys become. The one boy saw the mother's endurance, and vowed to himself that he was going to be a better father and a better example to his children. He saw the mothers' tears and that changed him. The other boy turned out to be just like the father. This father was given two gifts to shape and mentor for the next generation and he failed because alcohol robbed him of his purpose.

Experts say parent imitation/modeling is essential for children to develop healthy academic skills. If you want your child to become a reader, let her see you reading often at home. If you want a child to value learning, ask questions and learn new skills yourself. Model the behavior you want to see in your child. Say please and thank you. Your child might not say it right away, but she will over time. Make your rules match your expectations and your behavior. If you expect your child to put his dirty clothes in a hamper, you should do the same with yours. No parent is perfect all the time. If you do or say something you wish your child had not seen or heard, repair the interaction, and explain the consequences to your child. Explain to your child how what works in one place might not work in another. For example, loud voices are OK at the park, but not at the library. Explain why (Eliza Martinez, 20218).

Both marijuana and alcohol can have negative effects on a growing teenager's brain. It is important to know what is going on at school and among friends, to know what dangers they are facing, and to talk to them to warn them about the dangers.

Risky sexual behavior and activity

More than 50 percent of youths have had sex by the time they are 18 years old, according to the National Center for Health Statistics (NCHS).

Despite the recent drop in adolescent pregnancies, this does not always indicate that they are utilizing contraception: More than half of the 20 million new STD diagnoses each year impact people between the ages of 15 and 24.

Surveys regularly reveal that most parents do not believe their children are sexually active, despite the evidence. Again, even if you do not believe your children are having sex, it is crucial to talk to them about it.

Parenting A Teenager

How Can Parents Help Their Teenage Children?

First of all, we need to be present parents. Secondary we need to have a new perspective on who our teenagers are, get to know your children. Thirdly, the parents must know what their responsibilities are.

Right now, we need to stop whining and start looking for methods to support them. Parents need to improve their parenting techniques and take ownership of our teenagers. Parents must get involved in their children's lives.

We cannot shift our parenting responsibilities. They still depend on us, even if they are teenagers, just like they did when they were little. Their use of computers, smartphones, and other technological devices cannot provide kids with the nurturing they require. Let's stop allowing technology to raise our children. Parents must be present at home and at school, for example.

Better communication

Create channels of communication that are so strong that your kids will always see you as allies rather than foes. Avoid giving orders and using "I told you so" statements while communicating. During the discussion at home, as a parent, make sure they understand that you don't always have all the answers and that you're not always correct. Consider what they have to say and assist them if necessary. Give them room to express themselves, play the role of being a parent and a friend.

Set Rules/norms

Rules for housework, homework, driving, dating, sex, and drug and alcohol usage should be discussed and established. Continue to discuss each of these concerns with the children. House chores should be discussed and when they get time. Children must know that Saturdays are for cleaning up the house and doing laundry. They must be told to do the dishes and learn how to clean up after themselves. Children should learn that rules are the foster living habitants and strategies that will compel them to be better individuals.

Gratitude

Appreciate your children at every opportunity they have done well. This encourages them to do more and better. Tell them you love them and appreciate them. Our children go around thinking their parents hate them because all they hear from them is you did not do this and this or get this done now.

Outdoor activities

Take the children out of the house and go to the park, go for a driving adventure or go jogging with the children. During these activities the children feel love and they sometimes open up about their life struggles by themselves without having to ask. Create an environment where the child feels accommodated, and mommy or daddy is not going to judge me but will help me.

CHAPTER 9

Father's vs Daddy

What Is the Distinction Between a Dad and a Father?

You may have heard the saying, "Any man can be a father, but it takes a special man to be a Dad. But have you ever wondered that this terms "father" and "dad" are used to refer to a male parent.

Although they both formally imply the same thing, the definitions of what constitutes a father and what constitutes a dad sometimes differ.

This chapter delves further into the distinctions between a father and a dad as well as the real meaning of the words "father" and "dad." If you've heard the statement above and are curious about what it means, continue reading because I will give you all the explanations.

What It Means To Be A Father?

A father is anyone who can cause a pregnancy resulting in the birth of a child. This can be anyone, this is way you have teenage fathers, and aged fathers.

Although not usually their biological parent, some individuals refer to the man who raised them as their father as well.

Not All Fathers Are Dads

It is sometimes asserted that not all fathers are fathers. Right, it sounds perplexing. Any fertile man may father a kid, but becoming a father requires much more than simply conception.

The terms dad and father, particularly the word dad, stand for so much more than just a male parent. A dad is the man who raises you, loves you and is responsible for you while on the other hand, a father is your biological parent (he caused the pregnancy).

It can be perplexing because although the dictionary defines "dad" as the informal equivalent of the word "father," they might signify various things in different settings.

A father and a dad are not always the same, as society has long recognized. We are going to take a closer look at this as we go down the chapter.

Distinction Between A Dad And A Father

There are differences that exist between different father figures. A man might be a dad and something else, or just a dad. Don't worry if you sense that your brain is becoming a little confused; this chapter is here to clarify.

1. DNA

A father is a person who, together with your mother, was involved in your conception. A child will inherit genetic makeup and DNA from their father. This man can also be regarded as a dad if he decides to be present in his child's life and be a caring parent.

Father is a less common and less loving phrase than dad. We have more fathers present than dads. Because anyone can be a father but not everyone can be dad.

A dad does not necessarily have the same DNA as a child. The biological parents of a child is not invariably the dad. In some families, he serves as the father figure who raises the children's, provides for their needs, and loves and supports them.

Fathers don't always act in this way. You become a father when you conceive a child, but you become a child's dad when you take care of them and you are there for them every step of the way. Be it whether you can financially support or not. You need to be purposefully present.

2. Fatherhood is universal

Every living individual has had or now has a father. Unfortunately, a lot of children today grow up without dads. A man can "father" a child, but this does not make him a dad by default. (Davies, 2023).

Being a responsible and present parent is essential to being a dad. Although he could not even be aware that you were born, a dad will always be there for you. A father is given a birthright, but the label of Dad is something you earn by always being there for your kids.

3. Love

The sad reality is that not all fathers adore their offspring. Some children never get to meet their biological fathers, or if they do, they don't develop close bonds with them.

Not all fathers have an unwavering affection for their children's. However, a man becomes a dad by showing his children that he loves them without conditions and that he will always be there to assist them.

Without being a biological father, one can still be kind and capable of unconditional love.

4. Arriving/showing up

A father who is not around is still a father, but he isn't a dad. Dads attend their kid's soccer games, teach them how to ride a bike, assist them with schoolwork, and are proudly there at their graduation.

Dads do not allow their baby Mama relationships in cases where parties are not married to affect their relationship with the children. You might not be seeing your child's mother anymore, but as long as you show up for your children and show your love for them, you will always remain their dad. Even if you never send a birthday card, you must always make sure your children have the best and most amazing birthday.

3. Making memories

A father might be the biological father, the adoptive father, the stepfather, or even just a "father figure." Dads are very involved in their child's upbringing and are there in your cherished recollections of your family and upbringing.

Although they are aware that raising children is difficult, dads continue to be there, contributing to joyful family events and imparting important lessons that you will never forget.

You might not have any memorable interactions with your biological father if your dad is not your biological father.

Children raised only by their moms will not have any memory of their dads. However, if a mother later has a committed connection with another man, he might fill the role of the absent father in a child's upbringing and show them the affection they never had. However, that stepfather might only feel the gap of a father figure on the primary basis. If that stepfather becomes present in the child's life going the extra mile he can then further fill the gap of a dad.

Dads are caring and present, and they'll contribute to creating positive childhood memories, but this isn't always the case.

In conclusion, of this chapter, despite having nearly identical definitions, the words "father" and "dad" can indicate completely different things depending on the situation.

Any man may become a father, but not all fathers are good fathers. The term "dad" is sometimes regarded as being much more caring and loving, even if being called a "father" does not always imply that you are a horrible male parent.

Although every fertile man can become a parent, it requires dedication and love to be a dad. We hope this chapter has clarified the distinction between a father and a dad for you.

Dad	Father
A Dad will ask about your problems, and let you know he is there. Infect he goes to the extent of assisting to resolve your issue, either with you knowing or you not knowing.	If you have a problem, a Father may not care.

A Dad knows that respect is earned and should not be taken lightly.	A Father thinks that respect is due to him rightly.
A Dad will make time, no matter what else he has to do. A dad has time to check your books, make sure that your homework is done A dad is aware of your friend circle A dad shares in your trouble.	A Father may be too busy to take time to talk to you. A Father will be less likely to ask about your homework, assignments, friends, and challenges.

Your Dad can be a father, a best friend and in many cases go as far as taking the role and responsibility of the mother.	Your father is your father and that is it.
A dad is a role model.	A father is a father.

Dads and Son Bond

What Kind Of Bond Exists Between a Father and Son?

Sons and Daddies frequently have deep and tight bonds. They have a strong relationship that is based on love, trust, and respect. For their boys, dads frequently act as role models, showing them how to be strong and brave men. Sons look up to and respect their dads, seeking their advice and approval. In exchange, dads are happy to see their boys develop into maturity and are proud of them. This unique bond lasts forever.

The bond between a parent and son can be complicated. There may be friction and disagreement between dads and sons, yet sons may look to their fathers for leadership and support. Finding the ideal balance can be challenging, but a strong Dad-son bond is crucial for the well-being of both parties. It is ultimately up to each person to determine what works best for them among the various strategies to deepen the link between father and son.

Let's look at how you can strengthen your Dad-Son relationships/ bond:

Promote open dialogue: it's important to promote dialogue between a parent and son. This can help avoid misunderstandings and provide both parties an opportunity to honestly communicate their feelings to yield effective communication.

Spending time together: Spending time together is crucial for all relationships; however, it may benefit the father-son connection. Try to identify activities that you both like and schedule time to participate in them frequently.

Respect one another's differences: it is very normal and natural for a father and son to have different hobbies and viewpoints. It's just very important to accept one another's viewpoints and refrain from imposing your own on the other person.

Support one another: Strong relationships are based on mutual respect, trust, and support. Be there for your child when he needs you, and when it's appropriate, attempt to give him advice and direction.

Maintaining realistic expectations is important since nobody is flawless and father-son relationships may be challenging. Try to accept each other for who you are and try not to put too much pressure on yourself or your son.

Sons and fathers have a significant impact on one another's lives. You may both benefit from a solid and enduring tie by taking the time to maintain your relationship.

Now let's look at What Is The Bible's Teaching on Being a Good Father.

Being a good parent, according to the Bible, is crucial because dads have a big impact on their children's lives. They raise their kids with discipline, knowledge, and love, which helps them develop into responsible individuals. Fathers should spend time with their kids as well, getting to know them and encouraging spiritual development. Fathers are to be the leaders of their houses, according to the Bible, and they are to guide their families with knowledge, courage, and love.

Fathers, do not irritate your children; rather, raise them in the training and teaching of the Lord, as it says in Ephesians 6:4. According to this scripture, dads should not yell at their kids or try to discourage them. They ought to educate and train them in the ways of the Lord instead. This will assist children in becoming Godly, Christ-following adults as they mature.

"Train up a child in the way he should go, and when he is old he will not stray from it," says Proverbs 22:6. According to this passage, if we raise our children to follow the Lord from a young age, they will do the same when they get older. The values and lessons we instill in our children will stay with them for the rest of their lives because they will be deeply ingrained in their hearts and brains.

These rules I tell you today are to be in your hearts, according to Deuteronomy 6:6-7. Make an impression on your kids. When you are sitting at home, walking down the street, lying in bed, or getting out of bed, talk about them. According to this scripture, we should constantly discuss the Lord's instructions with our kids. When we are at home, on the move, or even just getting ready for bed or the morning, we should talk to them about this. This will enable them to constantly Maintain the Lord's instructions in their thoughts and hearts.

Fathers, you are incredibly important in the lives of your children. You serve as their role models, mentors, and instructors. According to the Bible, Dads should set a positive example for their children since children will imitate what they do and say.

For your children to see Christ in you, be sure that you are living a life that glorifies God. And make sure to spend time discussing the Lord with your kids so they can develop their faith and connection with Him.

If you came this far then Congratulations! it shows you are the next Dad out there.

Ten (10) Tips for becoming the Best Daddy

Be the "First Teacher" for your children.

1. Training a child in the way he/she should go is our responsibility. Not the government, not the school, but you— the father in particular (Proverbs 22:6).

2. Dads must serve as examples of a moral life (2 Corinthians 3:1–3).

According to the Bible, our lives and who we are serve as a "letter from God." That letter was read daily by our children.

3. Provide and Take care of your family (I Timothy 5:8).

Don't be too hard on yourself if you're having trouble finding a job. The heart and desire are more important in this concept. Being a good parent means more than just paying the bills. As fathers, we must see to it that all of our family's requirements are met. Even when it's difficult to provide for your family financially, try to find methods to do so.

4. Good parents instill discipline in their kids (Proverbs 13:24).

Scripture states that a parent who loves their child "is careful to discipline them." Proactive leadership in our families is another aspect of this.

5. According to Deuteronomy 6:6–9, fathers spend time with their kids; it is not idle time.

According to the Scriptures, fathers are required to have meaningful, in-depth interactions with their children that teach wisdom rather than just information. Plan some one-on-one "conversational walks" with your children regularly. Family time is what matters.

6. "Dad" traits include compassion.

A parent cares for his children. According to Psalm 103:13, "So the LORD has compassion."

7."Put your money where your mouth is"

Well, not quite in those words. But James 1:22 commands us to be "doers" of God's message as well as "hearers" of it.

8. Refrain from inciting your children (Ephesians 6:4). The Bible teaches that the better course of action is to raise children to be young believers.

Children who are aware of their fathers' daily prayers for them possess a strong sense of love and security.

9. Fathers never abandon their children.

In "The Prodigal Son" parable (Luke 15:20–24), a parent who never loses hope and is ready to welcome his child back with open arms is depicted. We may punish and hold people responsible, but we must never give up on them.

10. Fathers offer up prayers for their kids (1 Chronicles 29:19).

David the king prayed for Solomon, his son. Children who are certain that their fathers regularly pray for them possess a profound sense of love and security.

Chapter prayer points and meditation

Prayer Points:

1. Lord, give me strength and wisdom to raise my children in Your ways, with love and guidance. Help me be present in their lives and reflect Your love in my actions.

2. Lord, heal and restore the relationship between fathers and sons. Fill us with love, understanding, and forgiveness to strengthen our bond.

3. God, help me be the dad my children need—loving, attentive, and supportive. Teach me to lead by example and walk with them in faith.

Declarations:

<u>Book Tittle: Re Defining Manhood</u>

1. I declare I am a loving and responsible father, guiding my children with wisdom and raising them in God's ways.

   - Scripture: Proverbs 22:6

2. I declare my bond with my children is strong, filled with love, respect, and trust.

   - Scripture: Ephesians 6:4

3. I declare I will lead my family with love and wisdom, setting a godly example for my children.

   - Scripture: Deuteronomy 6:6-7

CHAPTER 10

Stepfather and Uncle as a Father Figure

Who is a stepfather?

A man, who marries a child's mother but is not the child's biological father (he is not a father by DNA) is known as a stepfather.

Can a stepfather be a dad?

Absolutely Yes! A stepfather can definitely be a dad in many meaningful ways. The role of a stepfather can vary depending on the family dynamics and relationships, but a stepfather can provide love, support, and guidance, much like a biological father. It often comes down to the connection and bond they build with their stepchildren. What's important is the effort and care they put into their role.

Why do children not respect their stepfathers?

We live in an error where children do not see or respect their stepfathers, children have Zero respect for them. **The question is why**?

Most men get involved with ladies who already have children but fail to become a father figure in the children's lives. They are only interested in their mother and forget that those kids are part of the mother. Of course, there will be resistance from the child at times, and I am not saying take the place of the biological father because you will never be able to. No price can ever be paid to replace the position of a biological father. But you can create your own special position as a stepfather. I don't mean that a stepfather will never be loved like or even better than the biological father, No! Quite the contrary. You can attain more favor in the sight of your step kids over their biological parents. But that should not be your mission. Provide genuine love and support as you will for your biological children, and stay within your lane because that's where you belong.

During a counseling session as a high school counselor, I was counseling a grade 10 learner, I asked if the child had a father the child said his dad passed on. I proceeded and asked, do you have a father figure in your life? The boy said NO!

I asked again, after the passing of your dad, did your mom get someone or she is just alone? The boy said, YES THERE IS A MAN IN MY MOM'S LIFE!

I asked, but is that not a father figure? the boy remained quiet. I proceed to question the boy, for how long is this guy in your moms life? To my surprise, the boy said they had been married for 5 years now…. The boy further explained why he was saying there was a guy in his mother's life and not in his life. The boy mentioned that the man only cares about his wife and not them, they don't even talk, they never sit at a table and talk, and they never even receive pocket money to go to school from him, hence they concluded that he is not a part of their lives.

Some men who become involved with women with children may indeed struggle to take on a father figure role. **There can be various reasons for this, including:**

Foolishness: some man's really lack wisdom, and they need to pray for it from God.

Uncertainty about Boundaries: Some stepfathers might not be sure how to navigate the boundaries between their role and the biological parent's role, which can make it challenging to form a strong bond with the children.

Resistance from Children: Children might resist accepting a new adult figure, especially if they're still processing the absence or changes related to their biological parent.

Complex Family Dynamics: Blending families often comes with complex dynamics that can make it harder for a stepfather to find his place and build a relationship with the children.

Differences in Parenting Styles: Differences in parenting philosophies or styles between the stepfather and the biological parent can create conflicts or confusion.

Personal Issues: The stepfather might have personal insecurities or issues that make it difficult for him to engage fully in a parental role.

It's important for all family members to communicate openly and work together to build positive relationships. Sometimes, professional counseling or family therapy can help in navigating these complexities and fostering stronger connections.

Winning the respect of stepchildren involves a blend of patience, empathy, and consistent effort. Here are some strategies a stepfather can use to build a positive relationship and earn respect:

Be Patient: Building trust and respect takes time. Don't rush the process or expect instant acceptance. Show that you're committed to being a positive part of their lives.

Respect Their Boundaries: Understand that children might need time to adjust to a new adult in their lives. Respect their space and let them come to you in their own time.

Communicate Openly: Foster open lines of communication. Listen to their thoughts and feelings without judgment, and express your own feelings and intentions honestly.

Build Genuine Relationships: Spend quality time with the children doing activities they enjoy. Get to know their interests, hobbies, and personalities. Building a bond based on shared experiences can help earn their respect.

Be Consistent: Consistency in your actions and decisions helps build trust. Be reliable, keep your promises, and maintain a stable presence in their lives.

Support the Biological Parent: Work with the biological parent to ensure you present a united front. Consistent parenting and discipline from both partners help avoid confusion and mixed signals.

Show Respect for Their Feelings: Acknowledge and validate their feelings about the family changes. Respecting their emotions and showing empathy can help build mutual respect.

Avoid Overstepping: Don't try to replace their biological parent or act as an authoritarian figure. Instead, find a balance where you can contribute positively without overstepping boundaries.

Demonstrate Integrity and Reliability: Show that you can be trusted to follow through on your commitments and that you have a strong moral compass. This can help establish you as a dependable and respectful adult in their lives.

Be a Positive Role Model: Exhibit behaviors and values you hope to instill in them. Actions often speak louder than words, so being a positive role model can influence their respect and admiration.

Seek Support if Needed: If challenges persist, consider family counseling or therapy to address underlying issues and improve relationships. Professional support can provide strategies for effective communication and relationship-building.

Building respect is a gradual process, but with genuine effort and patience, a stepfather can forge strong, positive relationships with his stepchildren.

Who is an uncle?

An uncle is a family member who is the brother of one's parent or the husband of one's aunt. In terms of family relationships:

Paternal or Maternal Uncle:

Paternal Uncle: The brother of one's father.

Maternal Uncle: The brother of one's mother.

Uncle by Marriage (In-Law Relationships): The husband of one's aunt (who is the sister of one's parent).

The responsibilities of an uncle can vary based on cultural norms, family expectations, and personal relationships, but generally include:

Supportive Presence: An uncle can provide emotional support and be a source of guidance and mentorship for nieces and nephews. This might involve offering advice, listening to their concerns, and being a positive role model.

Family Connection: An uncle often helps maintain family ties and traditions, contributing to a sense of family identity and continuity.

Occasional Caregiver: Depending on the family situation, an uncle might step in as a caregiver or help out with childcare, especially if the parents need assistance.

Role Model: Being a good role model in terms of behavior, values, and ethics can be an important part of an uncle's role. Setting a positive example for younger family members can influence their development.

Support for Parents: An uncle can support the parents by offering help or taking on responsibilities that lighten their load. This might include assisting with family events, providing financial support if needed, or simply being there to lend a hand.

Celebrating Milestones: Participating in and celebrating important family events such as birthdays, graduations, and holidays can be a way for an uncle to be actively involved in the lives of nieces and nephews.

Encouragement and Motivation: Encouraging and motivating nieces and nephews in their pursuits, whether academic, athletic, or personal, is another way an uncle can contribute positively.

While these responsibilities can be significant, the extent to which an uncle fulfills them often depends on individual family dynamics and the relationship between the uncle and his nieces and nephews.

Chapter prayer points and meditation

Prayer Point and Meditation

1. Lord, help me to be patient in building a relationship with my stepchildren. Give me wisdom to understand their needs and guide me in earning their trust and respect.

2. Heavenly Father, I pray for the strength to earn the respect of my stepchildren. Help me show genuine love, consistency, and integrity in my actions.

3. Lord, guide me in navigating the complexities of blended families. Give me the wisdom to know when to step in and when to support my partner in parenting.

Declarations:

1. I declare that I will be a positive and loving stepfather, providing guidance, support, and care, and fostering a strong bond with my stepchildren.

   - Scripture: Proverbs 22:6

2. I declare that I will be patient and understanding in building my relationship with my stepchildren, respecting their boundaries, and earning their trust.

   - Scripture: James 1:19

3. I declare that my blended family will grow in love and unity, with respect and understanding among all members, as we support each other.

   - Scripture: Ephesians 4:3

CHAPTER 12

Today's Current Job Market

On 19 March 2023, I was admitted to Okahandja state hospital, I was very grateful for the service rendered however, also very disappointed that all the doctors that attended to me from casualty, and emergency points to the male ward where I stayed for 42 hours were all females. All nurses are females.

What happened to the time when hospitals were dominated by Male Doctors alone? what is happening to this generation? The paramedics are females and even the person driving the hospital bus is a woman!! I cried seeing the male figures around the hospital burning the rubbish and cooking in the kitchen. I asked myself, what happened to the men of today?

You go to the town council the councils are dominated by Females, Okahandja has been governed by a female mayor for two consecutive terms. You go in schools women have taken over the management positions. Men are only after-school kids and alcohol. Where is the God-given dignity?

The parliament is flooded with women, and top positions in the cooperate are dominated by women. Most homeowners are women.

To make matters worse, even the incoming president is a woman! I am not against women in power, but I am against the drastic decrease of a male figures in leadership positions.

Where are we headed as a nation?

Men, we are losing our roles as heads. And for how long?

Reflection Questions to Men.

1. Has the rise of women in leadership roles exposed a deeper crisis in male identity and responsibility in society?

2. What will happen to future generations of boys if men continue to withdraw from their roles as leaders and providers?

3. Can we address the imbalance of male leadership without undermining the progress women have made in power, and if so, how?

CHAPTER 13

Manhood and Sexual Orientation

Biologically God only created a Male and a female. There is nothing such as others in God's creation. You can either be male with XY chromosomes or female with XX chromosomes. Unfortunately, many people leave in denial of their original biblical sexual orientation. In the biblical concept, there is no acceptance of things such as bisexuality, homosexual but acceptance is only made for individuals as desired from the beginning of creation. However today these terms are used by humans to please their satisfaction and as a means to justify their wrongs.

The moment you are an XY chromosome you are a man, (Male figure). Unfortunately, many most of the homosexual cases are a result of environmental factors from an early age. The devil then uses this opportunity to afflict them with sodomy spirit. However, when you find yourself in such a situation I want to remind you of what the bible tells us *"For sin shall not have dominion over you, for you are not under law but under grace."* Romans 6:14. The Bible also further says in 1 Corinthians 10:13, *"No temptation has overtaken you except such as is common to man; but God is faithful, who will not allow you to be tempted beyond what you are able, but with the temptation will also make*

the way of escape, that you may be able to bear it"

I came across many guys who refer to themselves as bisexual as I was doing research for this book. Some will tell you that they are attracted to the same gender. The moment they see them they are just attracted not knowing how. And there is another group that will tell you that the first time I slept with a guy had nothing to do with feelings but for the material benefit that I am getting.

However, from all the scenarios that I have been opportune to interview, I condemn no one, I judge no one! but still go back to the bible that God will never allow you in a temptation that you cannot overcome (1 Corinthians 10:13). NB! All it takes is self-discipline.

Napoleon Hill wrote a book on the power of the mind that whatever you feed your mind is what you become. It's important to choose what you feed your mind with!

In conclusion, in this chapter, I want to urge you to stand your ground as a man that God has created you to be and reject the act of homosexuality act. 1 Corinthians 6:9-11, 9 **Do you not know that the unrighteous will not inherit the kingdom of God? Do not be deceived. Neither fornicators, nor idolaters, nor adulterers, nor <u>homosexuals, nor sodomites,</u> 10 nor thieves, nor covetous, nor drunkards, nor revilers, nor extortioners will inherit the kingdom of God. 11 And such were some of you. But you were washed, but you were sanctified,** *but you were justified in the name of the Lord Jesus and by the Spirit of our God.*

A word to the future generation

Matthew 6:33 **"But seek first his kingdom and his righteousness, and all these things will be given to you as well"** in your walk with Jesus, embrace the journey with courage and integrity. The future is shaped by those who dare to dream and act with purpose. Be a beacon of resilience, kindness, and strength, for true manhood is defined by the positive impact you make on the world and those around you. Your actions today will forge the path for a brighter tomorrow, therefore lead with conviction, and never underestimate the power of your potential."

God Bless you!

ABOUT THE AUTHOR

Chief Andreas Robert

Andreas Robert is a dedicated advocate for boy-child empowerment, a passionate mentor, and a champion for health equity among adolescents. With over six years of experience mentoring boys, he has successfully established and led Boys' Clubs across Namibia, working tirelessly to ensure that no boy is left behind. His mission is to equip young men with the tools to lead, take up space, and embrace their God-given purpose in society.

Beyond his advocacy work, Andreas is an Apostle of God, entrepreneur, motivational speaker, life coach, author, and full-time high school counselor. He holds a degree from the University of Namibia and a theology degree from the Good News Theology School in the USA.

Born in northern Namibia and raised in the informal settlement of Five Rand Camp in Okahandja, Andreas understands the struggles of poverty, teenage pregnancies, and limited opportunities. These experiences fueled his commitment to uplifting young people, leading him to co-found the Hildes Women and Youth Empowerment Organization, a non-profit focused on mentoring and empowering Namibia's youth.

His impact extends beyond community initiatives. From 2020 to 2024, he served as a youth advisor to the Okahandja Town Council, advocating for youth development. His leadership in teenage pregnancy prevention campaigns across the country earned him recognition from UNESCO, where he contributed as a research assistant evaluating life skills programs. A SERAT Report by UNESCO under Mrs. Heitas office titled (FINDINGS FROM THE SEXUALITY EDUCATION REVIEW AND ASSESSMENT OF LIFE SKILL-BASED HEALTH EDUCATION IN NAMIBIAN SCHOOLS), where he evaluated the Namibian Life Skills curriculum to assess its alignment with international standards. He had the privilege of serving as the research assistant to Dr. Pandu Hailongo, who with his technical support, compiled the SERAT Report.

In 2025, Andreas was appointed as the new youth advisor for UNFPA Namibia (2025-2026), solidifying his role as a key voice in shaping policies for adolescent health, education, and leadership development.

Through his work, Andreas remains steadfast in his belief that men are called to lead, and he continues to expand Boys' Clubs in every town and village, ensuring that no boy grows up without guidance, mentorship, and a strong moral foundation.

Thank You for Reading!

Thank you for taking the time to read Re-Defining Manhood. I hope the insights shared have been inspiring and empowering for you. As you continue on your journey, I encourage you to live out the principles of true manhood-character, integrity, and courage-while impacting those around you positively.

Your feedback is incredibly valuable to me, and I would love to hear about your thoughts and how this book has made a difference in your life. Please feel free to share your review with me via email at chiefrobertofficial@gmail.com, or you can leave it on my website at: chiefrobertandreas.com .

Thank you once again for your support and for being a part of this movement.

With gratitude,

Andreas Robert

Boat of Salvation